I Love Pancakes

A Children's Tale

Roberta T. Glenn

Fulton Books, Inc.
Meadville, PA

Published by Fulton Books 2021

ISBN 978-1-63860-311-5 (paperback)
ISBN 978-1-63860-312-2 (digital)

This book is inspired and dedicated to my rainbow baby, Kendrick, as well as to all the mommies who love to cook for their beautiful children.

I love pancakes. I especially love it when Mommy makes them. They are so good! Oh, how I love pancakes.

Pancakes are my most favorite food.
I can eat pancakes for breakfast.

I can eat pancakes for lunch.

I can even eat pancakes for dinner.
Oh, how I love pancakes.

There are so many different ways I can eat pancakes.

BIG

SMALL

11

WHOLE

BITES

I can eat pancakes BIG, small, whole, or cut into bites.

I also can eat pancakes with my fingers or with a fork. Oh, how I love pancakes.

The best way for me to eat pancakes is with good ol' syrup and, of course, blueberries. Mmmm, so yummy. Oh, how I love pancakes.

But most of all, oh, how I love you too, Mommy!

The End

About the Author

Roberta Glenn is a first-time author. She is a believer in Christianity and a lover of all things in the '80s. Her passion for writing started as a young child growing up in Washington, DC. She now resides in North Carolina with her loving family.

CPSIA information can be obtained
at www.ICGtesting.com
Printed in the USA
BVHW021456070222
628303BV00018B/243

9 781638 603115